CRAFT BOX

Craft Like

THE ANCIENT EGYPTIANS

Jillian Powell

PowerKiDS press

Published in 2018 by **The Rosen Publishing Group, Inc.**
29 East 21st Street, New York, NY 10010

Cataloging-in-Publication Data

Names: Powell, Jillian.
Title: Craft like the ancient Egyptians / Jillian Powell.
Description: New York : Powerkids Press, 2018. | Series: Craft box | Includes index.
Identifiers: ISBN 9781499433692 (pbk.) | ISBN 9781499433654 (library bound) | ISBN 9781499433579 (6 pack)
Subjects: LCSH: Handicraft--Juvenile literature. | Egypt--Civilization--To 332 B.C.--Juvenile literature. | Egypt--
    Antiquities--Juvenile literature.
Classification: LCC DT61.P68 2018 | DDC 932.01--dc23

Editor: Elizabeth Brent
Designer: Rocket Design (East Anglia) Ltd
Craft stylist: Annalees Lim
Photographer: Simon Pask, N1 Studios
Proofreader/indexer: Susie Brooks

Picture acknowledgments: All step-by-step craft photography: Simon Pask, N1 Studios; images used
throughout for creative graphics: Shutterstock.

Manufactured in China
CPSIA Compliance Information: Batch #BS17PK: For Further Information contact
Rosen Publishing, New York, New York at 1-800-237-9932

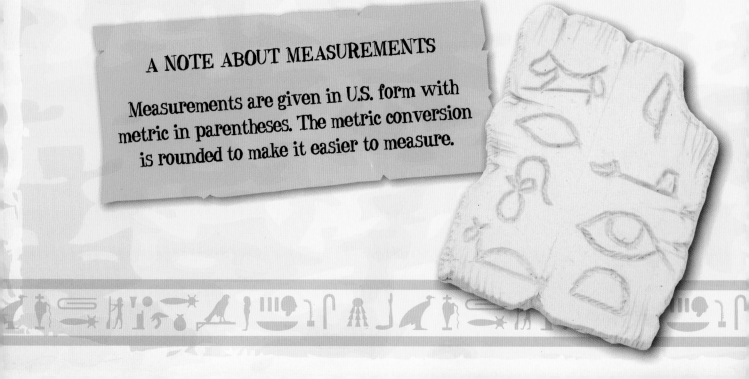

A NOTE ABOUT MEASUREMENTS

Measurements are given in U.S. form with metric in parentheses. The metric conversion is rounded to make it easier to measure.

Contents

the Ancient Egyptians

The golden mask of Pharaoh Tutankhamun

The ancient Egyptians lived along the Nile River. Each year, the river flooded, leaving a rich "Black Land" with **fertile** soil that brought them good harvests.

The ancient Egyptians lived from about 3500 BCE – 30 CE.

Ancient Egyptians were mostly farmers, but there were also **nobles**, **scribes**, and craftsmen.

Egyptian craftsmen were skilled metal workers, painters, carvers, and jewelers. They worked with stone from local **quarries**, **mineral pigments**, precious metals, and jewels from the desert they called the "Red Land."

Ancient Egyptians were great **architects** and **engineers**. They built huge stone pyramids as **tombs** for their kings, or pharaohs, and temples for the gods and goddesses they believed in.

Their beliefs and ideas were written by scribes on the walls of tombs and temples and on paper scrolls made from **papyrus**. They believed that there was an afterlife, or life after death. When Egyptians died, their bodies were mummified by **embalmers** so they were ready for the next life. Pharaohs' **mummies** were placed in tombs in pyramids, surrounded by all the things they would need in the afterlife.

These objects, from animal mummies to golden masks, can tell us lots of fascinating facts about life in ancient Egypt. They can also inspire you to make some Egyptian crafts of your own!

make a
Hieroglyphic stone

The ancient Egyptians used picture writing called hieroglyphics. They wrote in ink on papyrus or carved into stone. Hieroglyphs can stand for sounds or words. They can be read in different directions but always face towards the beginning of the line.

1 Work the clay with your hands to soften it, then flatten it into a slab about 1/2 inch (2 cm) thick.

2 Decide what you want your message to say. You could write your name or a secret word in hieroglyphs. You can find hieroglyphs to copy on page 30 or on the internet. Draw them on paper first to work out how big to make them and what your message will say.

3 Shape the clay into a rectangle then cut away bits to make it look like an old stone tablet that has been worn away.

4 Carve the hieroglyphs into the clay using the clay tools. Copy your drawings and make the marks as clear as you can.

5 Allow both sides of your stone to dry. Use the brush to seal the clay with a coat of white glue.

Did you know ...
Scribes had to learn and copy hieroglyphs at scribe schools. Army officers went to scribe schools so they could read messages sent to them.

make a
Pharaoh's mask

When pharaohs died, their mummies were placed in rich tombs. The mummies wore masks that looked like perfect, beautiful versions of the pharaohs' faces. These were made of wood, stone, or gold, like the golden mask of Pharaoh Tutankhamun.

1 Cut the rim away from half of the plate. Use the scissors to make slits for the eyes, then cut away the eye shape.

2 Glue or tape the fabric strips to either side of the back of the plate where the rim has been cut away.

3 Paint the plate and the cloth strips gold and allow them to dry.

4 Draw shapes like those below onto cardboard and cut them out. Make a vulture by folding a triangle in half down the middle. Fold the long sides of the big piece up, and stick the triangle between them to make the beak. Stick a circle on either side of the beak to form the eyes.

5 Paint the animal shapes, and allow them to dry.

Did you know ...
Ancient Egyptian goldsmiths made gold jewelry and used **gold leaf** to cover masks, furniture, tombs, and statues.

6 Decorate the edge of your mask with stripes and allow to dry. Draw a face onto your mask. Then make animals out of cardboard, paint them, and staple them to the top of the mask. Decorate the craft or lollipop stick and, when it is dry, tape it to the back of the mask to form a handle.

make an
Egyptian ∫ headband

Ancient Egyptian pharaohs and their queens wore headbands made from gold and decorated with precious stones to display their wealth and power. Headbands also kept headcloths and wigs in place.

1

Cut out a band of gold paper or card stock about 1 inch (3 cm) deep. It needs to be long enough to stretch around your head. Staple the ends together to form a ring.

2

Cut out a circle and a cobra shape. The cobra should be about 5 inches (12 cm) high.

3

Glue the circle to the middle of the headband, then glue the cobra to the circle.

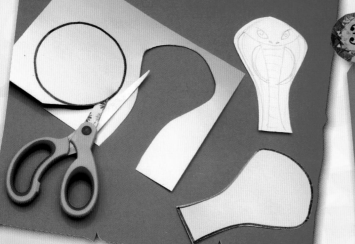

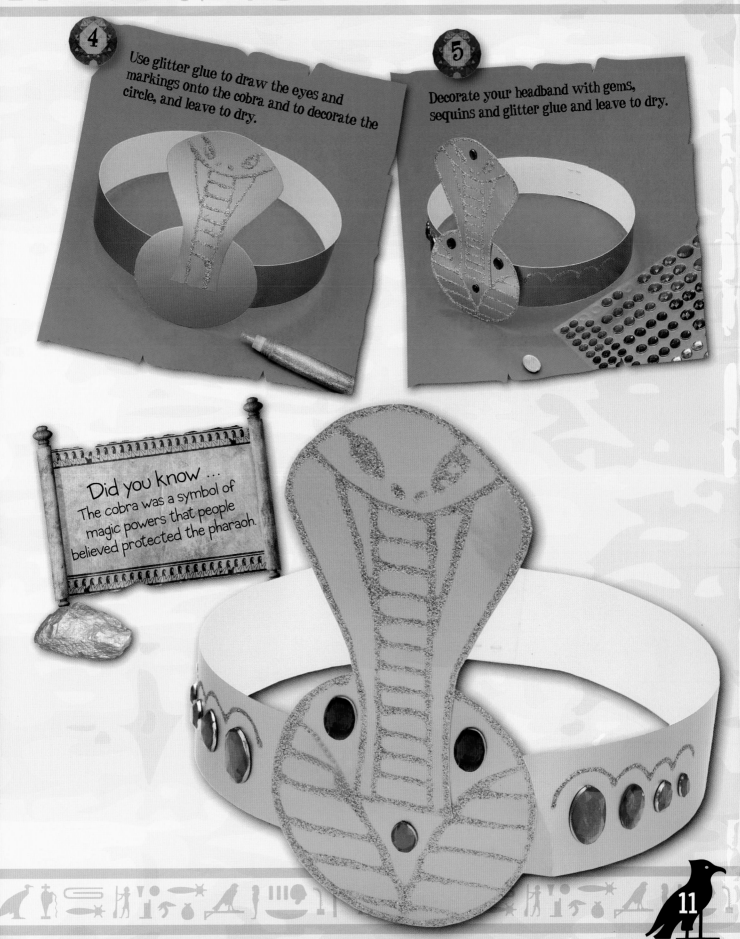

4 Use glitter glue to draw the eyes and markings onto the cobra and to decorate the circle, and leave to dry.

5 Decorate your headband with gems, sequins and glitter glue and leave to dry.

Did you know ...
The cobra was a symbol of magic powers that people believed protected the pharaoh.

make a
Scarab paperweight

The scarab, or dung beetle, was a sacred symbol to the ancient Egyptians. They used it on seals, **amulets**, and jewelry to represent the god Khephera and the rising sun, which they believed was re-born each day.

1 Take a piece of clay large enough to cover the stone and work it with your hands to soften it before rolling it flat using the rolling pin.

2 Wash and dry the stone, then brush one side with white glue. This will help the clay stick to the stone. Leave until the glue is tacky.

3 Sit the stone in the center of the clay, glue-side down, then brush the other side with glue, leave it to go tacky and wrap the clay around it. Mold it with your hands to form a smooth oval shape.

4 Use the clay tools to make the scarab markings. Look at pictures of scarabs in books or on the internet to give you ideas. When you mark out the body shape, cut away a small groove so you can paint these lines a different color from the body.

5 Mark a head and face onto the scarab using a clay tool.

Did you know ...
In ancient Egypt, scarab jewelry and lucky amulets were often given as gifts.

6 Allow the clay to dry, then paint with acrylic paints. When the paints are dry, brush on a coat of white glue to seal your paperweight.

make an
Egyptian armlet

Pharaohs and queens in ancient Egypt wore armlets as jewelry and for magical protection. Armlets were made from gold, silver and glass. They were often set with precious stones and carved with sacred names and symbols.

1 Cut the tube to the width you want your armlet to be, then cut the side open and try it on.

2 Cut two pieces of string long enough to go around your armlet and glue them around the edges. Cut more string and glue it around the armlet in scroll patterns.

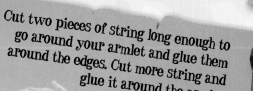

3 Cut out a cobra shape from the construction paper or spare cardboard.

4 Glue the cobra to the armlet so the head sticks up above the tube.

5 Paint the armlet with acrylic white paint and allow to dry.

6 Brush on the metallic paint. Cut out the eyes and tongue from construction paper and stick them on. Use the marker to add markings to your cobra or write names or other inscriptions. Decorate your armlet using glitter glue, paint or sequins.

Did you know ...
In ancient Egypt, armlets were worn around the wrist or upper arm.

make an Egyptian fan

Wealthy Egyptians had fan bearers to fan them in the heat. Fans were symbols of the breath of life, and of royalty and power. They were made from gold and **ebony**, precious stones, and ostrich feathers.

1 Fold one large and one small paper plate in half, and cut a slit in the bottom of each one for the craft stick or pencil to go through.

2 Fold the remaining paper plate in half and draw a shape like the one in the picture onto one side of it. Cut the shape out.

3 Push the pencil or craft stick through the slits in the bottom of the small, and then the large, plates. Tape the stick or pencil to one side of the large plate.

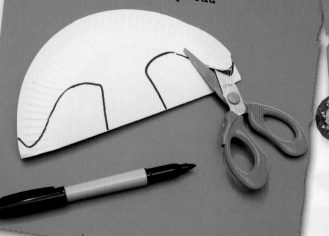

4 Cut a slit in the bottom of the shape you cut out in Step 2 and slide it on to the stick or pencil so that it sits on top of the small plate. Staple the shape to the small plate, paint the whole fan with metallic paint and leave to dry.

5 Glue the feathers between the open sides of the top plate, then glue the plate edges together. If you don't have real feathers, you can make paper ones.

Did you know ...
The ancient Egyptians used fans for **winnowing** and fanning incense during religious festivals.

6 Decorate your fan using glitter glue and small gems or sequins.

17

make a
Lucky amulet

The Egyptians carried charms, called amulets, to keep away bad spirits and to bring them luck. Amulets were placed between the layers of **linen** wrapped around mummies to keep them safe in the afterlife.

1

Look at some pictures of ancient Egyptian amulets in books or on the internet to give you ideas for shapes and colors. Sketch out a design for your amulet.

2 To make an amulet, take a small piece of clay and shape it using your hands, the rolling pin and the clay tools.

3

Push a paper clip into the clay to make a small hook.

4 Allow the clay to dry, then paint the amulet with acrylic or metallic paints. When the paint is dry, draw patterns onto the amulet using a marker.

5 Brush on a coat of white glue to seal and protect your amulet.

Did you know ...
Priests said magic spells as amulets were placed on a **mummy**.

6 Thread the cord or shoelace through the clasp to make your amulet into a pendant.

make
Egyptian wind chimes

The ancient Egyptians cast wind chimes from **bronze**. They may have used them to create music, to send away bad spirits or to forecast the weather.

1

Snip the rim of the cup to make triangle shapes, stopping about 2 inches (5 cm) from the base.

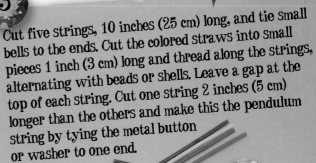

2

Paint the inside and the outside of the cup with acrylic paint.

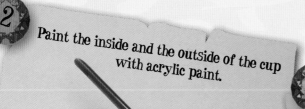

3

Cut five strings, 10 inches (25 cm) long, and tie small bells to the ends. Cut the colored straws into small pieces 1 inch (3 cm) long and thread along the strings, alternating with beads or shells. Leave a gap at the top of each string. Cut one string 2 inches (5 cm) longer than the others and make this the pendulum string by tying the metal button or washer to one end.

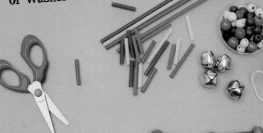

4

Pierce a hole in the top of the cup with a toothpick and, using a darning needle, thread the pendulum string through it. Make a loop in the string at the top of the pendulum that you can use to hang up your wind chime.

Did you know ...
The ancient Egyptians made mirrors by polishing bronze.

5

Pierce two holes for each of the remaining strings in the sides of the cup. Thread each string through two holes and knot inside.

6

Use a marker to decorate the sides of your wind chime with hieroglyphics or other patterns.

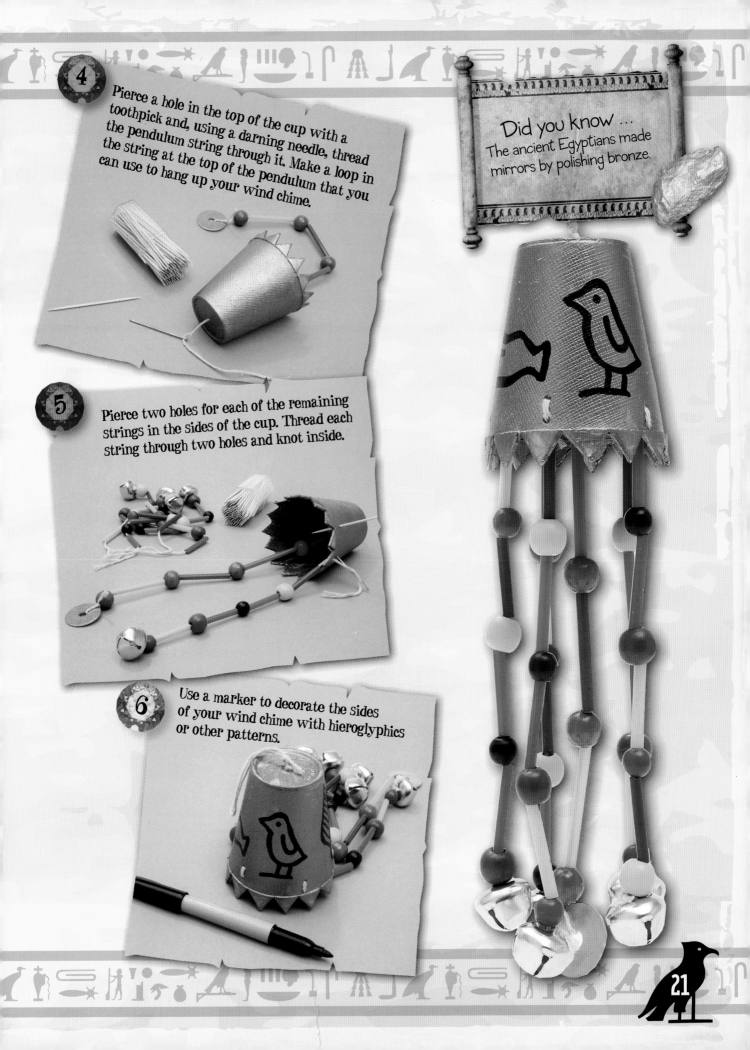

make a
Papyrus
scroll

Ancient Egyptians wrote on paper they made by weaving and pressing the **reeds** or stems of papyrus, a tall grass that grows by the river Nile.

You will need:
- Greaseproof paper
- White glue and water
- Acetate
- Sponge
- Tea or coffee
- Brown paper or card stock
- Sticky tape
- Marker

1 Tear the greaseproof paper into strips about 1/2 inch (2 cm) wide and 8 inches (20 cm) long. Mix some glue with the same amount of water.

2 Dip the paper strips in the glue mix and lay them on the acetate vertically, so the edges overlap. Repeat, this time laying the strips of paper horizontally to form a weave. Make a whole sheet of paper – uneven edges will help to make the scroll look old

3 Allow the glue to dry, then lightly brush or sponge on some tea or coffee that has cooled. Allow the paper to dry.

4

Make two tubes the same length as your piece of paper from brown paper or card stock.

5

Draw on some hieroglyphs. Look at pictures of ancient Egyptian scrolls in books and on the internet to give you ideas.

6

Carefully wind each end of the papyrus sheet around the paper tubes and glue or tape in place.

Did you know ...
The ancient Egyptians used papyrus to make everything from sandals to boats to mattresses.

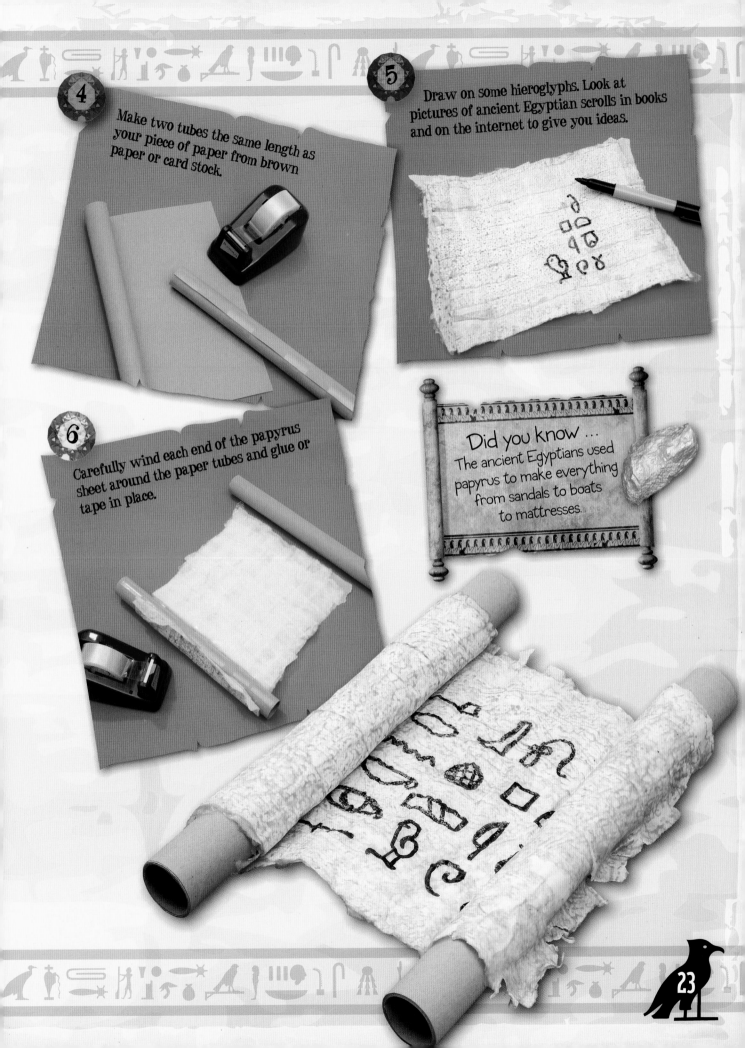

make a
Sarcophagus

Ancient Egyptian mummies were wrapped in linen and placed in a richly decorated coffin called a sarcophagus. It had magic spells written in hieroglyphics inside and out to protect the mummy in the afterlife.

You will need:
- Plastic shampoo bottle
- Paper cup
- Masking tape
- Tissue paper
- White glue and water
- Brushes
- Metallic and acrylic paints
- Marker
- Glitter glue

1 Make sure the bottle is clean and dry. Tape a paper cup onto the top, and a rolled-up piece of tissue paper to the bottom of the bottle.

2 Mix equal parts of white glue and water to make papier-mâché. Tear some tissue paper into strips, and begin laying them one way, then the other way, to make a criss-cross pattern. Repeat layers of papier-mâché to cover the bottle and create the shape of a sarcophagus.

3 When the papier-mâché is dry, brush on gold paint and allow it to dry.

4 Use a black marker to draw in the main body and head shapes and make two lines down the center of the body. Then draw hieroglyphics down this central band.

Did you know ...
Mummies were often placed in a "nest" of coffins, one inside another.

5 Decorate the sarcophagus with colors, using small zig-zags, triangles, stripes, and dots. Paint patterns in horizontal bands and use glitter glue for dots or egg shapes.

make
Animal mummies

The ancient Egyptians placed animal mummies in tombs, as they believed they would come back to life as pets for them in the afterlife. Animal mummies were also sold outside temples to be left as gifts for gods and goddesses.

You will need:
- Cardboard tube
- Paper cup
- Masking tape
- White glue and water
- Tissue paper
- Kitchen paper
- Brushes
- Marker
- Metallic paints
- White glue

1 Look at pictures of cat and dog mummies in books or on the internet to decide how you want your animal mummy to look. Choose a tube the size you want your animal mummy to be and stick a paper cup to the top of it with masking tape.

2 Push the sides of the cup down at one end to form ear shapes.

3 Mix equal parts of glue and water to make papier-mâché. Dip strips of tissue paper in the paste and smooth it onto the tube. Repeat, overlapping the pieces to form two or three layers in criss-cross patterns. Allow the papier-mâché to dry.

4 Soak pieces of kitchen paper in the glue mixture to make paper pulp, and then use it to shape a face on the mummy. Cover the paper pulp with a layer of papier-mâché to secure it.

5 When it is dry, paint the papier-mâché in silver or gold.

Did you know ...
Scientists have found mummies of cats, dogs, birds, **baboons**, and even crocodiles!

6 Use the marker to draw a face and markings onto your animal mummy.

make a 🐍 Lotus lantern

The lotus flower was an important symbol in ancient Egyptian religion. It represented the sun and re-birth because of the way the flowers close at night and open again with the sun in the morning.

1 Cut three cups into three different heights. You can use different-colored cups.

2 Snip away triangles from the edge of each cup to make petal shapes.

3 Place the tallest cup inside the medium cup, and then place them both inside the shortest cup. Gently bend each petal shape back to open up the flower.

4

Draw six leaf shapes onto the green card stock and cut them out.

5

Stick the leaves into the tinfoil case and then stick the case to the lid.

6

Write a wish on a piece of colored paper. You could use hieroglyphs to spell it out. Place the LED tea light in the middle of the flower, and tuck your wish in beside it. Light the tea light and set the wish lantern afloat.

Did you know ...
The ancient Egyptians used the lotus flower for herbal remedies and medicines.

Glossary

Amulet A lucky charm worn to keep evil or illness away.

Architect Someone who designs buildings.

Baboon A large, ground-dwelling monkey.

Bronze An orange-brown metal made from a mix of copper and tin.

Ebony An extremely hard, black wood.

Embalmer Someone who preserves dead bodies.

Engineer Someone who designs and builds the working parts of engines, machines or buildings.

Fertile When referring to land, this means that the soil is good for growing crops.

Gold leaf Gold that has been beaten or rolled into very thin sheets.

Linen A fabric made from a plant called flax.

Mineral pigment A dye made from minerals – naturally occurring substances.

Mummy A dead body that has been preserved in sand or ice or by embalming.

Noble Someone from a rich or important family.

Papyrus A reed-like plant that the Egyptians used to make sheets for writing on.

Quarry A place where stone is mined and excavated.

Reed A plant with a long, thin stem that grows near water.

Scribe A writer or scholar whose job was to write or to read.

Tomb A small building that acts as a grave, where someone's body is put when they die.

Winnowing Separating the outer husks from grain by fanning it.

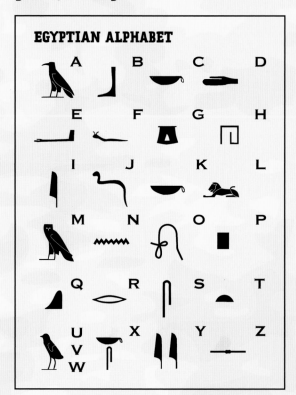

EGYPTIAN ALPHABET

Further information

BOOKS

Egyptology: Search for the Tomb of Osiris
Emily Sands and Dugald Steer
Candlewick, 2004

Everything Ancient Egypt
Crispin Boyer
National Geographic Children's Books, 2012

How I Became a Mummy
Leena Pekkalainen
The University in Cairo Press, 2016

WEBSITES

PowerKids Press has developed an online list of websites related to the subject of this book. This site is updated regularly. Please use this link to access the list:

www.powerkidslinks.com/cb/egyptians

Index

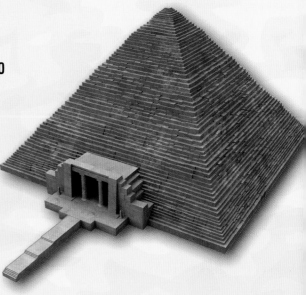